the Family Gratitude Project

Raise a Thankful Child with 52 Fun Activities and Crafts for Every Season

Joanna Grzeszczak

Ulysses Press

Published by:
Ulysses Press
P.O. Box 3440
Berkeley, CA 94703
www.ulyssespress.com

ISBN: 978-1-61243-839-9
Library of Congress Catalog Number: 2018944081

Printed in Canada by Marquis Book Printing
10 9 8 7 6 5 4 3 2 1

Acquisitions editor: Casie Vogel
Managing editor: Claire Chun
Project editor: Claire Sielaff
Editor: Lauren Harrison
Proofreader: Renee Rutledge
Front cover design: Ashley Pine
Interior design/layout: what!design @ whatweb.com
Photographs: © Joanna Grzeszczak

Distributed by Publishers Group West

IMPORTANT NOTE TO READERS: This book is independently authored and published and no sponsorship or endorsement of this book by, and no affiliation with, any trademarked brands or products mentioned or pictured within is claimed or suggested. All trademarks that appear in this book belong to their respective owners and are used here for informational purposes only. The author and publisher encourage readers to patronize the quality brands and products pictured and mentioned in this book.

To my daughters, Lilianne and Mila-Rose, my crafting companions, sweetest helpers, and imaginative co-creators of this book!

Contents

Introduction

As all busy moms and dads know, a lot of parenting is about sleepless nights, embracing imperfections, and making things up as you go! That's why this book is not about being a perfect "Pinterest" parent and it's not about raising an artistic genius. Forget about creating picture-perfect crafts—you already have enough stress in your life. You don't need to have any particular skill or talent to craft with your kids, and you don't even need a lot of energy. Most of these activities are designed for regular busy parents and regular crazy kids with short attention spans!

This book is for you to have a year of fun with your kids, a year of activities, laughs, and projects that will make you feel closer together, more grateful for your everyday lives, and thankful for each other.

You don't even need a craft room full of fancy equipment. All you need is a table to gather around, and a box or two with dollar-store supplies.

Why Focus on Gratitude?

Gratitude is an attitude and a way of thinking that benefits our health, satisfaction in life, relationships, and overall happiness. It is an important part of a mindful lifestyle because it helps us appreciate what we have instead of focusing on what we don't.

But gratitude isn't just for adults! By teaching kids to feel, embrace, and express thankfulness, we teach them to see the positives in life and to behave in positive ways. And this leads to fewer anxieties and more positive feelings such as joy, love, and happiness!

When I started this project with my kids, I realized that even though I tried hard not to "spoil" my daughters, they were not grateful for much in their lives. They would receive gifts and accept them like little princesses. Special outings and treats were another natural and expected thing for them. Even my husband didn't really see all the blessings that we had: a healthy family, a home to call our own, and a social circle around us. He'd compare himself to the ideal in his head instead and feel unsatisfied with his life.

But after doing these activities and projects together, something started to change. My kids started to say "thank you" after a meal or a simple walk to the park, and they were more excited by giving than getting. They'd ask if we could make a little gift for a family member or bring a special treat to our neighbors. My husband stopped constantly comparing himself with his friends and his ideas of what he "should" be and started appreciating his life more. As for me — an eternal optimist—I felt my heart grow with gratitude more than ever before.

Why Gratefulness Is Difficult

It's very easy for us to fall into the trap of negative thinking.

That's why working on a thankful approach to life is actually a very difficult mental exercise. It's hard to realize when anxieties and negative thoughts have taken control of our thought processes. But by focusing on the good things in our life, our achievements and the people who are there for us, we can push back against negative thoughts and habits.

By bringing gratitude into our everyday lives, we can feel happier, more satisfied, more connected to others, and more grounded in reality. Gratitude helps us focus on the positive, notice the little things, appreciate the efforts of those around us, and care for the environment and the natural world surrounding us. I believe that adopting this attitude and teaching it to our kids is one of the best things we can do for our families! And that's why this is a family project.

Through simple activities and crafts, we can teach our kids to have a grateful approach to life, as well as help them open their minds to positive thinking and a spirit of giving.

I hope that this book will help your family nurture a thankful home full of grateful hearts just like it did for mine!

Spring Projects

Potato Stamps

Potato stamps are one of those inexpensive crafts that you and your kids can do anything with—decorate a pillowcase, update an old tote bag, make a fun print, and more! This craft encourages kids to make a simple and fun print from scratch. The prints make excellent gifts for any person who has helped or encouraged your child this week.

My favorite potato stamp shape is a flower, but you can have fun and try making a heart, a tree, or whatever else you can imagine.

ALL YOU NEED:

large potato (russet or sweet)

knife

paint

plate

thick paper

frame

1. Start by cutting a clean potato in half. Then, carve out your shape. Remember that the face of the stamp should be flat and even, or else it won't translate evenly onto your paper. For safety reasons, you'll want to do this part yourself, especially if your children are younger.

2. When it's time to stamp, pour a little bit of paint on a plate, making sure not to use too much paint at a time. Stamp it onto the thick paper, or whatever surface you're using, to make your print.

3. Once the print is dry, it's time to frame it and gift it to a person that makes your kids feel grateful!

You can also try making prints by using lemons, apples, or pears cut in half. Just make sure that your lemon is on the dry side, or you'll be squeezing out the juice on paper instead of stamping it! You can also use other vegetables cut vertically, like okra, mushrooms, or peppers.

Gratitude Dream Catcher

Here's a fun decor craft that at the same time serves as a reminder to be grateful! It can be used as a bow and hair clip holder, a photo or note holder, or simply as a cute room decoration. As you can guess, I love little decor items like this, and the fact that it can serve multiple purposes makes it one of my favorite crafts!

The materials needed here are very similar to those for the Gratitude Mobile (page 49), so if you're going to buy an embroidery hoop for this project, you might as well pick up a few!

ALL YOU NEED:

embroidery hoop

lace ribbon or any other ribbon

glue or adhesive tape

scissors

embroidery thread in several colors

paper tags

pen

pompoms or bows (optional)

1. Remove the inside ring of the embroidery hoop, and set the outside ring aside for another use.

2. Wrap the wood hoop tightly with the ribbon. Tuck in the ribbon edges; if they don't want to hold, you can glue the ends down or secure them with adhesive tape.

3. Next, wrap the embroidery thread across the inside of the hoop. First tie one end and then start wrapping. Then, tie in the remaining end or trim the excess thread.

4. Next, take the tags and help your child write down who or what they are grateful for this week. Using embroidery thread, attach as many tags as you want.

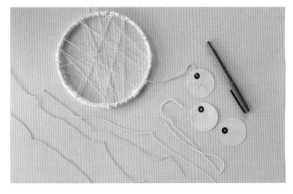

5. Using a different color thread, wrap some sections of the hoop to add more texture and color. We wanted ours to be pastel to match my girls' bedroom, but you can go for any color scheme you'd like!

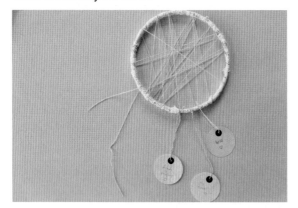

6. Braid some thread and attach the braids next to the tags for even more texture. You can also decorate it with more ribbons, pompoms, or even bows if you'd like. We chose to decorate ours with a small glitter bow for a bit of extra sparkle!

7. Hang the dream catcher in the bedroom as a reminder of gratitude.

Grateful Garden

Every spring my girls and I plant seeds. Some years it might just be one tomato seedling, while other years (when we are feeling motivated) we might plant all sorts of veggies and herbs. But every year we plant at least one seedling that we can later transfer to our backyard to watch it grow. I always prefer vegetables that are easy to sprout, like grape tomatoes, cucumbers, or zucchinis. These are all great for beginning gardeners and can be grown in pots if you don't have a yard. All they need is water and six to eight hours of direct sun every day. You can buy potting containers made for starting seeds at home; however, I've found that using regular grocery store egg cartons or toilet paper rolls cut in half works just as well and are much cheaper!

I call this a grateful garden because it teaches my kids how to patiently nurture something from start to finish. My girls also learn that by tending to their plants every day, they are important to that plant's existence. We jokingly say that the plant is grateful for the water and care it receives, so the gratitude goes both ways. If your kids are like mine, they might even name their plants—we find it makes for tastier zucchinis!

ALL YOU NEED:

potting containers or egg cartons	soil
scissors or knife	seeds

1. If you're using egg cartons, use scissors or a knife to poke small holes in the bottom of each compartment for drainage.

2. Add soil evenly to each compartment and slowly water the soil. You don't want to add a seed to the dry soil and then water it, or the seed will float up to the surface.

3. After the soil absorbs the water, it's time to plant the seeds. Make sure they are buried at a depth of around two times the width of the seed.

4. If your seeds are large, like sunflower seeds, put one in each section. If they are smaller seeds, two per section is fine.

5. Make sure to water the seeds each day, but don't overwater! Once they start germinating, teach your kids how to weed out the excessive and weaker sprouts. We normally keep eight out of a dozen.

6. Once the seedlings are 2 inches tall, you can plant them outside. Just make sure that the risk of ground frost is over in your region.

the Family Gratitude Project

Button-Flower Thank-You Cards

When I first started crafting, my older daughter, Lilianne, was around 18 months old. I remember I would get simple dollar-store kits of stickers and colorful foam shapes and have her play with them however she wanted—sticking them on a sheet of paper or on a toilet paper roll or all over her hands. The only rule was to stay at a table and not throw things on the floor, which is a big challenge for toddlers!

For me, this craft is a bit of a blast from the past, because it involves very little actual crafting and a lot of sticking. Paired with some simply drawn elements it results in a cheerful and cute handmade thank-you card for spring that your kids can gift with pride.

My girls don't need a special occasion to give out thank-you cards. Whether it's, "Thank you for going with me to the park," or "Thank you for coming over for dinner," I'm happy they enjoy expressing their gratitude. Even if the crafting is what they really enjoy, it's a good habit that I definitely encourage!

ALL YOU NEED:
colorful adhesive buttons
(or regular buttons and glue)

white cardstock

crayons

1. Stick colorful buttons on the card. Remember that they are the flowers, so you might want to encourage your children to stick them on at different heights, like how they would look growing in the garden.

2. Now draw the stems and the leaves.

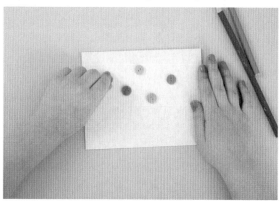

3. Add a thank-you note, and you're done!

DIY Scented Playdough

I believe that making handmade gifts is one of the best ways to express gratitude and have fun with your kids. And this playdough makes a great gift! You can put the playdough into small containers and have your kids give it to their friends, loved ones, and neighbors. Plus, homemade playdough is much cheaper than store bought, and the color and scent combinations are endless!

ALL YOU NEED:

1⅓ cups flour

2 tablespoons salt

2 tablespoons cream of tartar

medium bowl

spoon

2 tablespoons cooking oil

1 cup warm water

several smaller bowls

food coloring

essential oils of your choice (optional)

small saucepan or pot

1. Start by mixing the flour, salt, and cream of tartar together in a medium bowl.

2. Then, slowly add the oil and water, and mix it well until there are no lumps.

3. Separate the dough into smaller bowls if you want to make different colors.

4. Add one or two drops of food coloring (if you want a very saturated color, add three or four drops).

5. Add a drop of essential oil of your choice, if using (we went for lemon and lavender). Mix well.

6. Now it's time to cook the playdough. In a small pot over medium heat, slowly cook the dough while gently stirring with a wooden spoon. It may look like a disastrous lump, but don't worry—that means you need to keep on stirring!

7. Once the dough forms and you can't stir it anymore, it's ready. Just let it cool down before you pack it up or play with it. Refrigerate for up to two weeks.

the Family Gratitude Project

Tree of Gratitude

This project isn't about drawing a perfect tree. It's not about creating a piece of art either. It's simply about realizing the amount of support we have and appreciating all the people in our lives. So don't worry if you think you can't draw a tree, or if your kids are basically stamping everywhere but on the branches—it's all good.

ALL YOU NEED:

large colorful poster paper

pencils, markers, or pens

empty toilet paper roll

green paint

paper plate or something else to use as a paint palette

1. Start by drawing the trunk and branches of the tree on the poster paper.

2. Then, gently squeeze the toilet paper roll so instead of being round, it looks more like a leaf.

3. Using very little green paint at a time, stamp the leaves around the tree.

4. Once the leaves are dry, talk about all the people that support your family. Help your child name family and friends and write their names (or initials) inside the leaves. Hang it in a place where your kids can see all of the support your family has!

When I first did this activity with my younger daughter, she decided that the leaves should be flying around because it was a fall tree on a windy day. Believe me when I say that it looked nothing like a tree in the end! But we have filled her flying leaves with family members' initials, and we still felt so thankful when we saw the number of leaves filled with letters. Then, when we made this tree of gratitude again in early spring, she wanted all the leaves to be nicely growing from the branch. We even added two more leaves for our new neighbors! Sometimes it's not important how the craft turns out. What's more important is how it makes everyone feel—and both times we were happy in the end, which is exactly what I wish for you.

Nature Appreciation Walk

"Live in each season as it passes; breathe the air, drink the drink, taste the fruit, and resign yourself to the influence of the earth." — Henry David Thoreau

I really think that one of the best gifts we can give as parents is teaching our kids to appreciate and care for nature. It's important to foster a love for the outdoors in our children because being in nature is good for us! It soothes, calms, and can even help with anxiety. This nature appreciation walk activity helps kids concentrate on the nature around them, encouraging them to look for details and to see all the beautiful things nature has to offer, whatever the season.

ALL YOU NEED:

Nature Appreciation Walk printable

pencil or pen

drawing paper (optional)

colored pens or pencils (optional)

digital camera (optional)

Go for a walk in your backyard, at a park, or on the beach with your list of things that your child needs to find on a walk. For older kids, encourage them to make drawings or take photos of each of the items they found, and then create a nature appreciation album out of it. You could even ask them to write an essay about appreciation of nature.

We went for our nature appreciation walk in springtime, and after months of cold weather and snow, my girls loved discovering all the little spring details that forest had to offer! Whatever the season, I hope that this activity will help you, too, see more details out in nature and appreciate our beautiful world.

Tip: To get you started on a list, I have prepared four different "hunt" printables for each season, available at http://www.lazymomsblog.com/gratitude-printables.

the Family Gratitude Project

Body Positivity Poster

With the prevalence of photoshopped and unattainable bodies constantly being portrayed in the media, it's more important than ever to instill in our kids positive body images and self-love. From a mindfulness perspective, it's really important to teach kids to focus less on how they look and more on what they can do, as well as to worry less about how others see their bodies and to think instead about how they feel inside their bodies. So of course this book wouldn't be complete without at least one activity encouraging body appreciation!

This activity can be made in two different ways. With little kids, the focus is on teaching them the functions of their bodies and showing them how amazing their bodies are. Older kids, however, can be encouraged to draw how they see their own bodies. And then asked to describe every part in a positive way only: without talking about how it looks, but what it does and what it lets them do in life. Both older and younger kids can talk about why they are grateful for their bodies in general too.

In both scenarios I encourage *you*, the parent, to sit with your kids and talk about how amazing your body is as well! Research also shows that moms who show to their daughters that they love and accept their own bodies are the ones who raise body-positive kids. And if a dad chips in his own perspective on body appreciation, it also helps!

ALL YOU NEED:

colorful cardstock or construction paper

scissors

marker

glue

1. Draw a shape of a person on one piece of cardstock, cut it out using the scissors, and glue it on another big piece of cardstock.

2. Now draw arrows pointing at different body parts.

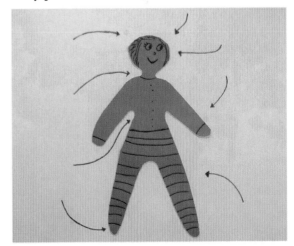

3. Cut out small rectangles from the remaining cardstock and glue them around the arrows.

4. Now fill in the rectangles with descriptions. Ask your kids to describe their body in a positive way, responding to these questions:

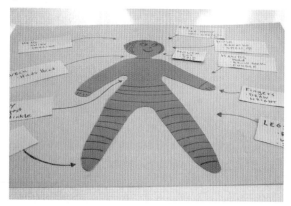

What does you body do for you?

Why is this body part important?

Why is your body amazing?

What does your body let you do in life?

With smaller children, focus on general bodily functions and ask them what they can do thanks to them.

5. Once finished, hang it by the closet where your kids dress, for a reminder of how amazing their bodies are.

the Family Gratitude Project

Thankfulness Coloring Pages

The theme for these coloring pages is all the little things in a child's life, like animals and imaginary creatures, smiles and cuddles, ice cream and sunshine, rainbows and summer rains. Little things that make them smile and appreciate the everyday.

Part of this activity is to actually talk about all the little things that make your kids feel grateful in their everyday lives. Maybe your kids are like mine and are thankful for their cat's purrs and their sibling's kisses. It can be as small as watching ants in the sun—one of my younger daughter's favorite little things! Whatever it is, take time to talk about those simple moments while your children color. And if your kids are a bit older and enjoy drawing on their own, you can encourage them to draw their own version of "thankful for the little things" coloring pages. The easiest way to turn a drawing into a coloring page is by scanning and printing it out for others to enjoy.

"Thankful for the little things" can also become a daily mental exercise for you and your kids, because while not every day is great, there is something great in every day! Find these coloring printables at: http://www.lazymomsblog.com/gratitude-printables.

Paper Wind Spinners

This super-simple craft shows kids how to turn humble materials into pretty decor pieces that look lovely with just a little help from nature: wind. I had to include this classic craft project in my book, and with a gratitude spin (pun intended) they turn into a perfect spring craft.

I love the metaphor behind wind spinners: All the good things that influence us and make us feel grateful are spinning around each other, creating even more good and positivity!

Last but not least, this is a great fine motor skills exercise for younger kids.

ALL YOU NEED:
colorful craft paper

pen

scissors

colorful pipe cleaners

1. Start by drawing large spirals of various sizes on the craft paper. The more spirals you draw inside the circle, the longer your wind spinner will be, so take that into consideration if you don't have tall trees to hang them on.

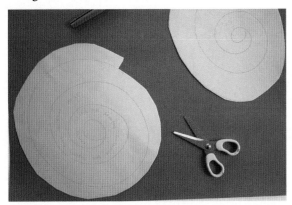

2. Talk with your kids about what they feel grateful for this week, and then help them write it down on the spiral.

3. Now it's time to cut the spiral out, leaving a small circular space at the top for attaching the pipe cleaners.

4. Make a small hole with the pointy tip of the pipe-cleaner and then attach it to your spiral. The other side will serve as a hook.

5. Unfold your wind spinners and go hang them on the tree in your backyard or by the window!

Rainbow Raindrops

This craft is all about teaching kids perspective and how it relates to gratitude. It's easy even for us adults to see only one side of the coin, so I found this activity to be a fun reminder—as much for myself as for my daughters—that what seems to be annoying at first can actually bring us joy later on.

So here's the spring rain metaphor: Kids may be sad when it rains since they can't play outside. But if they're patient and wait until the storm ends, they get to go out and splash in puddles. They might even get to see a rainbow! In the end they'll feel grateful and happy for that spring storm that made them feel sad in the first place.

This craft then turns into a cute wall decoration that's perfect for your kids' room. We hung ours in the girls' playroom, and we talked some more about how we are grateful for spring rain, not only because it brings gorgeous rainbows and puddles to play in, but also because it waters the gardens and brings water into the lakes and rivers for the animals and humans to enjoy.

ALL YOU NEED:

white sheet of paper

marker or pencil

scissors

colorful crayons

blue sheet of paper

thin ribbon

glue or adhesive tape

1. Start by drawing a rainbow shape on the white sheet of paper (use a stencil if you prefer).

2. Cut the rainbow out, and color it in with crayons.

3. Next, draw raindrops on a blue sheet of paper, and cut them all out.

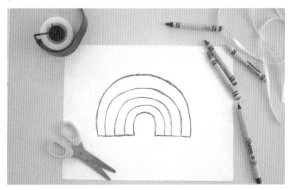

4. Cut the ribbon in strips and attach them to the back of the rainbow. You can use glue or tape, whichever you prefer.

5. Turn your rainbow colorful-side up and glue the raindrops onto the ribbons.

the Family Gratitude Project

Giving Back "Cookie Jar"

This fun craft is centered around teaching kids that it's good to give and it feels good to help.

After making your cookie jar, you can sit down with your kids and write down small (or big) acts of kindness that they did for someone else that day. Do this every night around dinnertime so that by the end of the week you'll have a jar full of "cookies." Nothing is too small to write on a cookie, whether it be helping a sibling get dressed in the morning, doing a chore without being asked, or even giving someone a feel-better hug!

At the end the week, your child can take all the cookies out, and together you can read aloud all of the good actions. This creates a great opportunity for you and your kids to talk about how they felt when they did something kind for someone else, as well as the importance of giving back or helping out without being asked.

ALL YOU NEED:

brown sheets of paper

permanent marker

scissors

empty jar

ribbons

paper tag

pen

1. Start by drawing the cookies on brown paper. The circles don't have to be perfect!

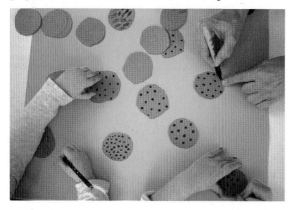

2. Now, cut out the cookies and draw black dots for chocolate chips. (This is a great fine motor skills activity for preschoolers!)

3. Decorate your jar with ribbon and label it with a paper tag.

4. Put all the cookies (and a pen, so you won't have to look for it later) in the jar. Keep the cookie jar on the kitchen table; keeping it in sight will make it easier to encourage your kids to talk about the acts of kindness they did, and after a couple of days it will make them more motivated to actually do more kind things and to write on more cookies! It may also make you feel like baking cookies, but hey, I warned you!

Since this book is based on a whole year, all the learning is happening over time. Throughout this book you'll find different activities centered around giving back. This craft is another great exercise that will help your kids discover how they can be kind to others in everyday situations.

Summer Projects

Gift a Plant

Do you remember those little sprouts that we planted in our Grateful Garden (page 15)? They should be ready now to repot! And if, like us, you planted all of the seeds from your seed packet, then most likely now you have 10 to 14 baby zucchinis, tomatoes, or cucumbers. Unless you live on a good-sized piece of land, this is way too many plants of the same sort for a small backyard garden, not to mention a humble patio pot.

So it's time to part with more than half of your baby plants, which is great, because sharing is caring! Every time we show up unexpectedly at a neighbor's door with a small gift, it teaches our kids the power of giving back and encourages them to think about others more often.

To gift your plants, you'll need to put them into bigger pots. Ideally this can be done starting from when a seedling grows its second set of true leaves. Also, in order to make sure they can be planted outside, you'll need to "harden" the seedlings, which means getting them out in the sun and wind for a couple of days before repotting them.

I usually put seedlings out on the patio for an hour or two on the first day, and then for a full day the next two days, and then once the frost risk is over, I leave them out for a night or two. And only then do I replant them directly to the garden or into bigger pots for the patio.

HOW TO TRANSPLANT SEEDLINGS:

1. Prepare the new pots. We use medium-sized plastic pots for gifting, as the rest of our seedlings are going in our garden.

2. Fill the pots up two-thirds of the way with fresh, moist soil.

3. Gently pull apart the seedling from its container, preferably with your fingers, but you can use a blunt knife too. Just make sure you're not destroying the roots.

4. Next, gently place the seedling in the middle of the new pot, and then surround it with more soil.

5. Gently press the soil around it.

6. Water the plant and the soil to collapse any air pockets.

And voilà! The plant is ready to be gifted.

Colorful Nature Hunt

"Mere color, unspoiled by meaning, and unallied with definite form, can speak to the soul in a thousand different ways."—Oscar Wilde

So here's a summer family activity that turns an ordinary walk into a fun and thankful nature hunt! As Oscar Wilde said, colors "speak to the soul," so this activity is all about encouraging kids to appreciate colors and textures in nature—and reminding ourselves of this too. Rocks, flowers, feathers, or birds' eggs, anything that's colorful and can be found in nature counts!

Here are a couple of ideas on how to use the printable, which is available for download at http://www.lazymomsblog.com/gratitude-printables:

💜 If your kids are on the younger side, you can simply print the colorful nature hunt page and let them cross each color off the list every time they find a matching colorful object.

💜 Or, you can tell your kids to collect tiny objects like flowers, feathers, or rocks, and stick them to the printable once you're back home—just don't try collecting birds' eggs as mama birds would be upset!

💜 After the walk, you can ask your kids to draw the colorful nature objects that they found.

💜 You can print more than one page per child, and ask them to look for only flowers for the first page, then only rocks, then only animals, and so on.

💜 If your kids are a bit older and know how to use a camera, you can ask them to prepare a photo journal of what they found.

💜 If they are on the preteen side and you'd like them to participate in this activity too, ask your kids to make a short video with music about all the colorful things that they spotted during the hunt. Songs like "What a Wonderful World" would be a good fit, or maybe they can even make their own song.

Just remember, if you're going to any type of national park, it's best to either draw or make photos of the things that you found, and leave everything in nature intact.

You can find the colorful nature hunt page at the link on the previous page, or you can prepare one on your own. Simply write down the colors on one side of the page and leave empty squares on the other, so your kids can check them off the list. I hope you'll have as much fun as we did!

Ice Pop Garland

Popsicles are one of my kids' favorite things about summer. But there's so much more to appreciate about the season than just sweet treats. So to help my girls realize all of the other things they love about summer, I helped them make this adorable ice pop garland!

This banner makes for a fun bedroom or playroom decor addition, plus it's so simple to make. We used paint swatches from the hardware store, because if you think about it, they usually already look like fruity ice pops!

ALL YOU NEED:

4 different colors of paint swatches

scissors

brown crafting or construction paper

glue

pen

white string

small clothespins

1. Start by choosing your ice pop flavors, aka colors. Depending on the length of your paint swatches, you might want to trim off one or two colors.

2. Cut out ice pop stick shapes from the brown paper.

3. Now it's time to glue the sticks to the ice pops!

4. After the ice pops have dried a little, talk with your kids about all of the things they love about summer. These could range from little things like ladybugs to big memories like a trip to the waterpark or a fireworks show. Either you or your child can write them on the back of each ice pop. My kids found they were most grateful for camping trips, spending time with their grandparents, and of course, ice pops in the afternoon!

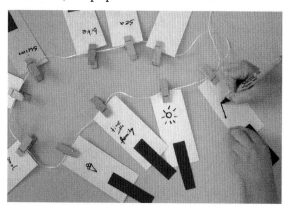

5. After each ice pop has its own note of gratitude, hang them along the string using small clothespins. (This is great fine motor skills practice for smaller kids!)

6. Once the banner is all done, you can help your kids hang it up so they'll always be reminded of all the wonderful things they appreciate about summer.

the Family Gratitude Project

Thankful Time Capsule

Putting together a time capsule and burying it in the garden is a magical childhood experience that you can easily organize at home. Leaving memories of the present time and then finding those messages again years in the future makes for an unforgettable family activity. And of course, it's also a great opportunity to help everyone feel grateful for the present and thankful for the past all at once.

Your family can put anything inside the time capsule, whether it be little objects that have marked your summer, notes of what each family member is grateful for, or even family portraits.

Here are some other things that you might want to include in your time capsule:

💙 A list of current family members including pets, with everyone's age.

💙 A family photo.

💙 A colorful piece of paper with notes on what each member of the family is grateful for this summer.

💙 Kids' drawings of what they are grateful for/family portrait/someone they love.

- 💜 Kids' handprints, traced on paper with a crayon or stamped with paint.

- 💜 Notes about family members' favorite toys, colors, or snacks.

- 💜 Tickets from family activities to remember.

- 💜 Written stories about family memories.

- 💜 A question that can be answered only in six months to a year, for example:

  - ❥ What will my next school year be like?
  - ❥ Who will my teacher be?
  - ❥ Will we have another baby in the family?

  - ❥ Will the new baby have dark or pale hair?
  - ❥ Will X lose their front teeth?
  - ❥ Will Y learn to ride a bike?
  - ❥ Where will we go for vacation?
  - ❥ Are we going to get a pet?

- 💜 A nice secret, a good gesture, or an act of kindness.

- 💜 Little messages for each child from parents or for each parent from children.

You can use a glass container, a plastic bottle, or a little box secured in a large zip-top bag. I suggest burying it not too deep in the ground and in a place that will be easy to find the following year, like in the corner of a garden, underneath a tree or underneath the front door steps. If you don't have a garden to bury it in, I suggest putting everything in a box, with a sign reading "Don't open until XXXX," securing it with duct tape, and hiding it deep in the closet!

Gratefulness Cootie Catcher

Cootie catchers are another easy and inexpensive way to have fun. The best thing about them is that they only require a piece of paper, a pen, and a bit of imagination!

I decided to put a grateful spin on this old classic, and even created a template for you to use! If you have more than one kid, make sure to print more than one so each child can have his or her own cootie catcher.

Here's how it works: After folding your cootie catcher, you choose a sibling, a family member, or a friend to play, and have them say a number from one to 10. You open up and down and side to side as you count to the number they picked. When you've stopped counting, leave it open and ask: "Up or down?" Unfold the flap they chose and read the question there aloud. Of course, all questions are about gratitude!

HERE'S HOW TO MAKE YOUR COOTIE CATCHER:

1. Print out the Cootie Catcher template, which you can find on my website here: http://www .lazymomsblog.com/gratitude-printables.

2. Then, fold the paper in half to make a crease. Unfold, and fold again along the other side.

3. Now flip the paper so that the white side is facing you. Fold all four corners toward the middle.

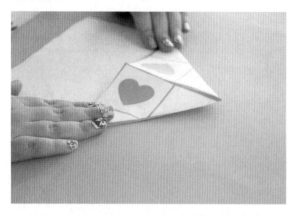

4. Flip again, white side forward. Fold the four corners toward the middle again.

5. Fold it in half (the side with text will stay inside).

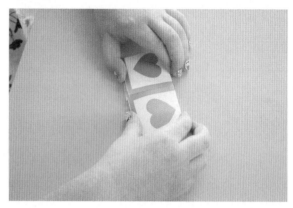

6. Push your fingers into the square pockets and push the flaps up to open the cootie catcher.

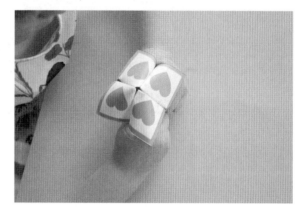

Thankful Yoga Session

Yoga has long been something I want to do more of and something I want my kids to learn too. And while we're definitely far from being yogis, we do love how convenient it is. You can practice yoga anywhere and at any time. There's no special equipment needed and it teaches kids to focus, concentrate, and be aware of their bodies!

So here's a simple yoga routine for expressing gratefulness for many aspects of nature:

First, to remember the poses, my kids and I came up with this rhyme:

"I love nature, sun, and trees, animals big and small, and all the little seeds."

I usually recite this rhyme with my kids, and while slowly saying it, we enter into the following poses:

1. Start by saying hello to the sun (stand tall with your feet together and hands wide above your head), then do the tree pose (put your hands together above your head, and put one foot on the other while keeping your balance).

2. Next, do the cat and cow poses (from your hands and knees, drop your belly and look up for cow pose, and then arch your back up like an angry cat for the cat pose).

3. Now it's time to do the cobra pose (while lying down on your stomach with legs stretched out, place your hands directly under your shoulders and lift your head, shoulders, and chest off the floor and arch the back).

4. End with the seed pose, aka child's pose (sit back on your heels and slowly fold forward, bringing your chest to your thighs and your forehead to the ground; breathe slowly and rest).

If you too are a yoga newbie, don't worry if what you're doing is not perfect—this activity is about connecting with each other and expressing thankfulness for nature, and not about achieving perfection!

the Family Gratitude Project

Gratitude Mobile

Even though mobiles are usually associated with nurseries, I think they are just as cute in older kids' rooms! They add a bit of sculptural interest, dimension, and movement without taking up any floor or wall space. Plus, they're so fun and easy to make with your kids.

We went for a fish theme because it's summer, and when I asked Lili and Rose what animals they associate with summer, they said fish in the ocean. But you can do whatever shapes you want! You can also personalize your colors to fit your kids' rooms.

ALL YOU NEED:

paper tags with holes

scissors

pen

medium-sized wooden embroidery hoop

colorful embroidery thread

1. If you want your mobile to look like ours with the colorful fish, then cut the first tag out into a fish shape, leaving the hole as an eye. Then, use this first fish as a stencil to cut out other fish. You can also cut out hearts, starfish, seashells, or simple circles.

2. Once you have enough paper fish or other shapes to hang, write on one side of each of them all the summer activities, moments, and memories that you and your children are thankful for.

3. Next, tie one end of a piece of thread through each fish's eye and the other end to the embroidery hoop. Use different colors and lengths of thread to vary the heights once they are hung.

4. Keep tying the tags all around the hoop.

5. Finally, attach a string on opposite points of the hoop so you can hang it from the ceiling. We hung ours over my girls' beds, though if you have a covered porch then it would also look lovely there moving with the wind!

Surprise Stones

One thing my kids love about summer is park season. Our weekly strolls to the park play such a big role in their social lives: This is where they make new friends and where they meet with our neighbors. So, of course, it's only natural that we wanted to bring a bit of sunshine (or should I say, a rainbow) to our local park and find a simple way to give back to our community.

Since everyone loves surprises and hidden treasures, we decided that painting rocks and hiding them around the park for kids to discover would be the best way to share our gratitude. With this craft my girls got to express their own gratitude for their local community, and they got to surprise other kids with a small token of thankfulness as well.

ALL YOU NEED:

smooth rocks

colorful paint

small paint brushes

permanent marker

1. First, get outside with your kids and collect some rocks. Make sure the stones are smooth enough to be painted and have at least one flat side. Also, don't use rocks that are too small, as they may be a choking hazard! Be sure to wash the rocks before painting.

2. Paint rainbows on the stones using small paint brushes, and remember, it doesn't have to be perfect to make someone smile!

3. You can add simple messages with a permanent marker on the other side of the stones too. We chose to write "Be grateful," "Love more," "U R loved," and my personal favorite, "You rock!"

4. Let the rocks dry completely and then take them to your local park. Your children can hide them behind tree stumps and in the bushes, under the slides, and underneath the benches. Skip the baby section of the park though; it's better if older kids find your gratitude stones!

Paper Watermelon Thank-You Cards

Making your own thank-you cards is a great way to teach kids to express their gratitude to family and friends. These cheerful watermelon cards are perfect for any summertime thank-you note!

My four-year-old, Rose, made these cards to thank her friends for inviting her to a pool party. This craft is great for all ages—even toddlers—it just requires Mom or Dad to help out with some cutting.

ALL YOU NEED:

pink, green, and white cardstock

glue

scissors

empty white cards

permanent marker

1. Start by cutting the watermelon shape out of your colored cardstock. I piled mine one on top of another, starting with white, then green, and then pink, and holding on to one corner, I cut the other side into a round shape. Then, I trimmed it to look more like a watermelon slice. Just remember to keep in mind that the green paper slice should be the biggest one as it peeks out from underneath, and the pink piece should be the smallest.

2. Once that is done, don't forget to draw the watermelon seeds on the pink paper with a permanent marker.

3. After the seeds have been drawn, it's time to glue the pieces together to make a watermelon slice!

4. Now write "Thank you" on another piece of pink or green cardstock and cut it out. For a more laid-back look, carefully rip it out like we did. You could even write, "Thank you for being so sweet," for a card with a punny punch!

5. Glue a watermelon slice and your thank-you message onto the front of a white card.

the Family Gratitude Project

The note holders display:
- THANK YOU FOR MAKING ME SMILE TODAY!
- I'M SO THANKFUL FOR YOUR FRIENDSHIP!
- THANK YOU FOR BEING SUCH A GREAT FRIEND!

Colorful Animal Note Holders

Here's an idea for another fun craft to help kids express their gratitude for friendships. My girls loved transforming simple dollar-store animals into these colorful and cute note holders. (These could also be used as photo holders if you prefer.)

While this craft is fairly simple and needs only a couple of layers of paint and glitter, it does require the help of an adult with a Dremel tool.

ALL YOU'LL NEED:

plastic animals

water-based acrylic craft paint

paint brushes

glitter powder

Dremel tool

1. First, paint the animals with craft paint. Depending on the colors you're using, you might need to do two coats for even coverage.

2. After the final layer of paint, add colorful accents like contrasting socks, or colorful ears and tails. While the paint is still wet you can add glitter too—because everything is more fun with glitter! Just make sure that you shake off any excess.

3. Allow the animals to dry completely.

4. Once the animals are dry, use a Dremel tool to cut a horizontal slot on the animal's back for the note card.

5. Once the animal note holders are all done, encourage your kids to think of who would get excited about receiving a gift like this and what they can write on the note for that person. You could also use School Notes for Friends (page 68), like we did. Or you can print out a photo instead of a note. Either way, these little jungle friends make perfect friendship gifts!

Ladybug Rocks

There is so much to be grateful for in the summer. Flowers, how food grows, and the little garden creatures that help in pollination are all things to be thankful for during the season.

That's why this craft is all about teaching kids to respect little bugs such as ladybugs and bees, and helping them understand how important they are in the garden and in nature in general. My girls loved painting these little bugs, and then playing with them in our backyard, hiding them in pots, and grouping them into families.

ALL YOU NEED:

medium-sized smooth rocks

water-based acrylic paint

small paint brushes

1. Start by painting an off-center line on a rock, and then paint the larger side a color of your choice (the unpainted part will be the head of your bug). We painted colorful ladybugs and yellow bees, but if your kids want to paint purple or blue bugs, then why not!

2. While the body of the bug is drying, paint the "head" black and add black or white dots for ladybugs and black stripes for bees.

3. When everything is dry, paint their eyes.

4. Once your rock ladybugs and bees are all dry, it's time to hide them around the garden or in the pots with plants! It's a good moment to talk about how pollination wouldn't happen without little helpers such as bees, ladybugs, butterflies, ants, and beetles, and how it's important to let them live and do their jobs.

Tip: If you want the rocks to be able to stay out in the rain all summer long and not risk damaging them, you should cover them with a water-resistant coating.

Gratitude Tic-Tac-Toe Kits

Tic-tac-toe is such a classic. And no wonder: It has easy rules that even a young child can follow, needs no special materials, and helps kids develop strategic thinking and planning. This DIY felt version makes for a great portable game kit that easily fits in a pocket or small bag. Plus, with the gratitude spin on the rules, it helps children express thankfulness!

HOW TO PLAY:

Each of the players has one set of shapes. Taking turns, players place their shapes in the empty boxes on the board. With every move each player makes, they say one thing for which they are grateful that day. The player that has put all of their shapes in one line—be it diagonal, vertical, or horizontal—wins.

ALL YOU NEED:

colorful felt sheets

scissors

adhesive jute tape

1. Start by cutting the felt sheets into squares.

2. Then, cut the jute tape into thin strips. You'll need four strips per tic-tac-toe board.

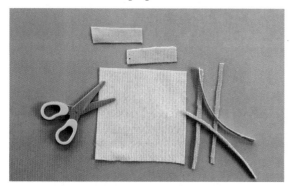

3. Next, decide what shapes you'll be playing with. Since it's gratitude tic-tac-toe, we decided that each set needs one set of hearts in it. But hearts can be difficult to cut for a preschooler, so we also added squares, triangles, and crosses. I think that mixing shapes looks even cuter. So go with whatever shapes you and your kids like! Just remember, you'll need two different sets of three matching shapes for each kit.

4. Finally, stick the jute adhesive tape to your felt squares (you need nine equal-sized squares).

5. Once your kits are all done, fold a couple of kits with their shapes nicely tucked inside. Wrap them with another jute tape string and a little felt bow, then give to your friends or loved ones!

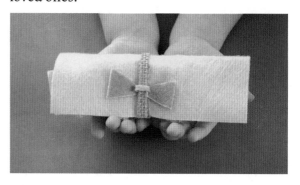

the Family Gratitude Project

Rainbow of Emotions Garland

Paper garlands are one of the most timeless crafts, and kids of all ages love to make them. This project takes the classic garland and adds a new twist to help kids learn about their emotions. Through making their own Rainbow of Emotions, your child will learn how each and every emotion is important, as well as how to be grateful for the emotions that they feel—even the negative ones! It's important for kids to understand and express their emotions because it helps them appreciate their own thoughts and feelings, something that gratitude is all about. From sadness to joy, this craft will help your child grow closer to their emotions.

ALL YOU NEED:

colorful construction paper

pen

scissors

rope

small clothespins

1. Start by folding a sheet of paper in half, and then draw a triangle, keeping the folded side intact at the bottom.

2. Then, use that first triangle as your stencil to draw and cut out the other colors.

3. Choose one emotion for each color, and write it down on one side of each garland piece.

4. Then, on the other side of the garland piece, write what good may have come from that feeling, why your child felt that way, or why in the end it was good to have had that emotion.

5. Attach each banner on the rope using a clothespin and hang up your child's finished garland on the wall as a reminder of all the emotions that we should be grateful for.

When Lili and I made this garland, I asked her first to tell me which color made her think of which emotion. As we worked through the craft, I helped her think about how each emotion might have helped her do, think, or feel something positive in the end. For instance, when she told me about feeling sad, we talked through that emotion and discovered she had felt sad because she missed her grandma. Though sadness isn't a good feeling, Lili found it created a positive result because it motivated her to call her grandma and then make her a pretty card. This craft helped Lili express her thoughts, and it also helped her realize that expressing her feelings is a good thing!

Fall Projects

Gratitude November Rains

My kids dislike rain. I find this funny because I prefer a cozy day indoors during a rainstorm over a cold snow day outside! But kids are kids. They want to play outside, and they can't do that when it's raining. So I think that rain is a great metaphor to talk to kids about their attitudes toward difficulties and problems. It's important to teach them that some challenges lead to closer connections and new solutions!

This rainy-day activity is all about that: finding a positive aspect of a difficult situation and appreciating the people who helped us through difficult moments. It could also be a great springtime activity as well.

ALL YOU NEED:

2 or 3 shades of blue watercolor paint	pen
watercolor paper	scissors
paint brushes	tape

the Family Gratitude Project

1. With very little watercolor paint and a lot of water, let your kids play with brushstrokes until an entire page of watercolor paper is covered with different shades of blue.

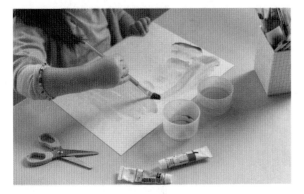

2. Let the painting dry, and then let your children draw raindrops on it with a pen.

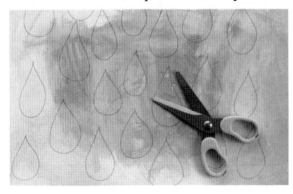

3. Cut the raindrops out.

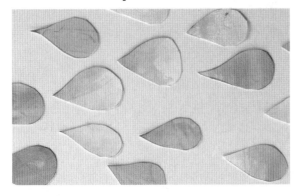

4. If your kids are a bit older, ask them to tell you about a recent struggle, a dispute they had, a difficulty at home or at school, or a fear. Then, help them find a positive of that situation: Was there something they learned? Was there a person who helped them? Was there a new solution they found?

5. Ask them to write the positives on the raindrops, then tape the finished raindrops to the window.

6. If your kids are younger, simply ask them who helped them recently. Whether it was their sister who helped with putting on shoes or Dad teaching them to spell, ask them what was difficult about the situation and how they felt after they got help. Together write the name of a person who helped them (or just initials), and then tape the finished raindrops to the window.

7. You can also stick empty raindrops on the wall or refrigerator, and then fill them in during the week. The more raindrops there are, the bigger the proof that even when things don't go as planned, there's always something to be grateful for!

Thankfulness Branch

Do your kids enjoy decorating the Christmas tree? Mine love it! The problem is that it's only a once-a-year opportunity, and they also have a mom who has her own opinion of how the Christmas tree should look, so they can't really do it entirely as they'd like.

But I did let them hang note tags on this fall branch in any way that they wanted, and they said it was as much fun as decorating a Christmas tree! They even started singing Christmas carols.

This activity is a simple way to count all the things that your family is grateful for this month. There's plenty of space for everyone to add additional thoughts throughout the month, and it also makes for a lovely fall centerpiece.

ALL YOU NEED:

tree branches

large vase

tags

pen

1. Cut some tree branches and place them in a vase.

2. Hang tags on the branches and set up a pen station next to it.

3. Every evening at dinnertime, ask everyone around the table to share what made them feel grateful that day. Was it someone helping them, or was it something they accomplished or learned? Maybe they are grateful for playing a fun game or something small, like enjoying their favorite lunch. Whatever it is, add it to the thankfulness branch.

4. At the end of the month, take the notes down and put them in an envelope. Seal it, write the date on top, and put it in your souvenir box (or in another safe place like your kitchen drawer). Open it next year around the beginning of the same month. Read the notes aloud together before starting another thankfulness branch.

School Notes for Friends

When my daughter Lili was starting school, I remember how worried I was! I wondered if she'd like her teacher, if she'd adjust to the new routine, and most importantly, if she would make good friends.

Thankfully she did (that's something that I'm grateful for), and now she loves going to school. But maintaining friendships is not always easy for her, and saying the right thing at the right time is still something she's working on. But when she comes home and tells me stories about her friends, I can tell she's thankful that they are in her life.

So to help her express this, we came up with a variety of colorful printable school notes.

💜 Thank you for being such a great friend!

💜 Thank you for making me smile today!

💜 Thank you for always making me laugh!

💜 Thank you for having my back!

💜 I'm so thankful for your friendship!

the Family Gratitude Project

You can print these messages at home using the templates on my website http://www
.lazymomsblog.com/gratitude-printables.

Or if you prefer, you can encourage your kid to handwrite their own messages on a piece
of cardstock.

Depending on your school rules, here are some ideas on how your child can surprise their
friends with the note:

💜 Stick the note to a fruit snack.

💜 Tape it to a pretty set of pens.

💜 Leave it in your friend's backpack or pen case.

💜 Put it in an envelope and give it to them directly.

No matter how the note is given, expressing gratitude for a friend not only strengthens
that relationship, but it also makes both the giver and the receiver feel good about
themselves. This is what it's all about!

Q-Tip Dot Tree Thank-You Cards

Fall may be one of our favorite seasons. The crisp air, the golden light, apple picking, pumpkin carving, and beautiful colorful leaves—so many things to be grateful for! Playing with colorful fall leaves is my kids' favorite autumn activity, which I used as inspiration for these cards.

Giving back and expressing gratitude is a big part of the *Family Gratitude Project*. That's why these thank-you cards are such a great project. Plus, not only are these easy enough for a child of any age to make, but the crafting also helps develop fine motor skills and patience.

ALL YOU NEED:

colorful cardstock

scissors

brown marker or crayon

orange and red paint

plastic bowl

Q-tips

glue

1. First choose a fall color for your card. We went for bright yellow. Cut out the rectangle for the card, draw a tree trunk in the middle, and color it in. For younger kids you can trace a circle (the tree canopy) so they'll know where the painting limit is.

2. Pour a bit of each color of paint into a small plastic bowl.

3. Start with one color: Dip a Q-tip in paint and gently press paint dots inside the canopy circle.

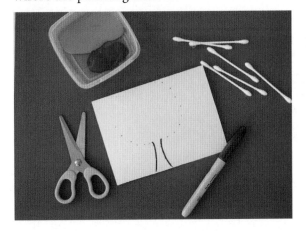

4. Then, add the second color of dots.

5. Once the tree looks like it's full of colorful leaves, let the card dry.

6. Meanwhile, write your thank-you note on a piece of complementary-colored cardstock (we chose orange).

7. Gently tear the note out and glue it on top of the card.

Tip: You can encourage older kids to make a thank-you Q-tip card with three trees instead of one, all with different fall leaves colors.

Upcycled Apples

Teaching my kids that it's possible to make something pretty and cute out of nothing is what I love the most about crafting with them. This upcycled apple project is such a great example of that. It shows that sometimes all you need is to take something out of the recycling bin, and add some craft paper, patience, and a bit of imagination—and voilà, you end up with the cutest paper apples that add an adorable autumnal touch to your home!

ALL YOU NEED:

scissors

red construction paper

green construction paper

pen

empty toilet paper rolls

glue

1. First, cut out long strips—about ¾ inch wide and 8 inches long—of red craft paper. You'll need six to seven strips per apple.

2. Next, cut out "leaves" from the green crafting paper. We used two per apple.

3. Now, talk with your kids about fall activities and how they enrich your family routine. Ask your kids what they are thankful for in this season. Write their ideas down on the red paper strips.

4. Cut out a long, wide strip of red paper, wrap it around the toilet paper roll, and glue it down to cover the cardboard.

5. Start gluing the strips into each side of the toilet paper roll one by one. Help your kids by pressing the strips against the roll tightly so they hold.

6. After the red strips are secure, glue the tip of each leaf into the roll as well.

Now it's time to go and pick some real apples! Just don't forget to bake a pie after and give one to your neighbor too.

Gratitude Conversation Starters

We all know that eating dinner together as a family is important. It's when we catch up with each other, talk about our days, unwind, and share our struggles and victories.

But family dinners are not always picture perfect—young kids may be too sleepy to participate and simply cry and misbehave, older kids might respond with only "good" and "I don't know" to any questions asked, and parents may be too tired to even initiate a family conversation.

That's why I prepared these gratitude conversation starters. For younger kids it may be a distraction from their dinnertime whining, for older kids it can be a game of questions, and for adults it provides an easier way to find that family connection once again.

Here are 25 questions to start a conversation, some focusing on helping one another, some on gratitude, and some on the day's events.

- What are you the most thankful for today?
- Why are you thankful for your family?
- Who helped you today?
- Who are you grateful for today?
- What are you grateful for in nature?
- Who was kind to you today?
- What have you learned today?
- Who made you smile today?
- Who did you help today?
- What is something that always cheers you up?
- Who were you kind to today?
- What made you happy today?
- Who did you laugh with today?
- What little thing made today a good day?
- What obstacle did you overcome today?
- What activities did you enjoy the most today?

- What is something you love about your mom?
- What sort of beautiful things did you see today?
- What did you do today to help someone have a better day?
- Why are you grateful for this day?
- What is something you love about your home?
- What did your family help you with today?
- What is something you love about your dad?
- How did you helped your family today?
- What is something you love about your sibling?

Just remember, it's not supposed to be an interview, but a way to start a conversation and reconnect around dinnertime! See where the topics take you. You don't have to follow them strictly and can of course ignore the rest of the questions if a great conversation comes up. For a printable version of these 25 questions, go to http://www.lazymomsblog .com/gratitude-printables.

ALL YOU NEED:

Gratitude Jar Conversation Starters template

scissors

heavy cardstock (optional)

Mason jar

colorful washi tape

ribbon

1. Start by printing out the Gratitude Jar Conversation Starters template, then cut out the questions. If you'd like, print out the questions on heavy cardstock so that the paper slips last longer. You can also write down the questions yourself.

2. Decorate the mason jar with colorful washi tape and ribbon. This can be the job for the youngest one in the family!

3. Place the conversation starter jar on your kitchen table, and every evening at dinnertime, let each member of the family pick their own question to answer from the jar. Alternatively, every evening let a new family member draw one question for everyone to answer.

Either way, try to have fun, laugh, and talk to each other!

the Family Gratitude Project

Jack Straws Game

Do you remember playing jack straws when you were little? It used to be one of these simple yet very engaging social games that kids of all ages loved. You had to be patient, persevering, and very, very careful. It was definitely one of my favorites!

So I decided to make a small twist on this classic game and introduce it to my kids. First, we made our own straws out of small sticks that we found in our backyard. Second, I added a gratitude rule.

But before we get to the rules, here's how you can make your own game.

ALL YOU NEED:

small sticks

scissors

colorful acrylic crafting paint

paint brush

1. Gather sticks in your yard or on your next trip to the park. They should be all the same thickness, but don't worry if some are longer than others—you can always trim them a bit. I suggest around 20 sticks for two players, so if you have three or four kids, you might want to collect more sticks than we did.

2. Trim the sticks to be approximately similar in size, but leave the small bumps. They don't have to be all the same; in fact, it makes for a more interesting game if they're not.

3. Paint the sticks in the colors of the rainbow! Just make sure you have the same number of each color in the end.

4. Once they are dry, you're ready to play!

HERE ARE THE RULES:

Dump the stick straws on the table. Each player needs to take a stick from the pile without moving any other sticks. If they succeed, they keep it and they say one thing they are grateful for, then they try again. If they move any stick other than the one they try to pull out, their turn is over, and then it is the next player's turn. Keep playing until all the sticks are gone. The winner is the person with the most sticks.

If your kids are a bit older, you can also count points: for example, four points for yellow, three for pink, two for blue, and one for green. In that case, the winner would be the one with the highest number of points!

Whichever set of rules you choose, I hope you'll have as much fun as we did!

A to Z Blessings Game

Do you ever play car games? We do, since we have family living almost 250 miles away from us, and we spend quite some time on the road. One of the games that we play while on the road is the A to Z game. It's about naming animals, cities, or food starting with all the letters in the alphabet. Not only is it a great game to build vocabulary and learn the alphabet, but it's also a fun game to play at home on a rainy day! It's also a perfect way to foster a conversation about gratitude with your kids.

We played this game on a Sunday afternoon and upped the stakes by creating two teams: my husband and Lili against me and Rose. I must admit, finding a thing I was grateful for that starts with X was a bit challenging!

HOW TO PLAY:

Print out the A to Z form from my website at http://www.lazymomsblog.com/gratitude-printables, or write down the alphabet in a line, leaving space for your blessings. Give a form to each player.

Ask everyone to write down what they are grateful for: one person, thing, or event for each letter. The winner is the person who finishes first.

If your kids are younger and are just starting to write or can't write just yet, you can agree on five to eight letters to fill in, and play with an adult and a child on each team.

Most importantly, have fun, and good luck with coming up with ideas for X!

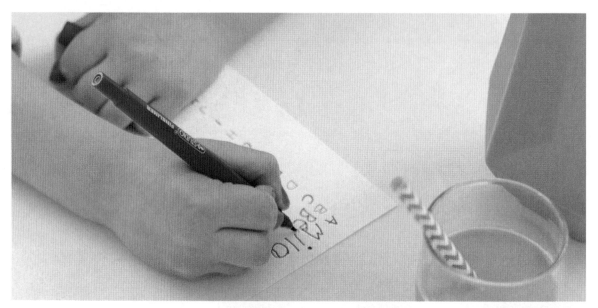

the Family Gratitude Project

DIY Frames

As the saying goes, a picture is worth a thousand words, and what's better than a picture of something or someone you're grateful for in a little DIY frame?

These frames are made out of very humble materials and they are easy to put together. Plus, they make changing images very easy—no glass frame in the way! They also make for cute gifts or bedroom decor, which basically means that they are the best type of craft: cheap, cute, easy, and multifunctional!

ALL YOU NEED:

cardboard

scissors

pen

adhesive tape

colorful washi tape

crayons

photo

1. Start by cutting two identical squares out of the cardboard. Set one square aside; this will be the back of your frame.

2. Now draw a ¾-inch border around the second square and cut the inside out, only leaving the edge; this will be the front of your frame. Don't worry if it's not perfect!

3. Using adhesive tape, stick the two pieces of the frame together, leaving one side open. Remember that you need to leave space on one side for sliding in the photo.

4. Next, decorate the frames with washi tape.

5. Finally, add a little stand to the back of the frame by cutting out a small a piece of cardboard, bending it slightly, and sticking it onto the back with tape.

6. Now, the frame is ready to use. Ask your kids if they want to draw what they are grateful for this week, or if they want to find a photo of the person or the relationship that makes them feel thankful.

the Family Gratitude Project

Rose decided to put in one of the frames a photo of her as a baby with her sister because she said she's grateful for her big sis (of course this melted my heart right away). Then she said she's also grateful for her great-aunt who invited her for a sleepover, so she drew her portrait and then gifted it to her. And that's how, with one little craft, Rose made three people smile: me, her sister, and her great-aunt.

Grateful for the Seasons Poster

This activity is definitely not about making a perfect poster, so don't worry if no one in your family is an artist. The purpose of this activity is to simply realize how lucky we are that the seasons exist, how grateful we are for each one of them, and how every season—even your least favorite—has family activities and moments that we can be grateful for.

Older kids will enjoy doing the poster from A to Z, while younger kids will love painting the trees and telling you what they appreciate the most in each season.

ALL YOU NEED:

large colorful cardboard

pens

sticker letters

paint

glitter paint

paint brushes

paper

glue

1. Start by drawing four trees on the cardboard. They can be as simple as a rectangle for the trunk and a big circle for the canopy of leaves.

2. Use the sticker letters to write, "Grateful for the seasons," or anything else to express your family's thankfulness for the changing seasons.

3. Paint the trees with regular paint and glitter paint leaves according to the season. We used light green for spring, darker green for summer, yellow and orange for fall, and white for winter.

4. Now it's time to brainstorm and write down all the things that make a season special for your family. Write them on little pieces of paper and glue the papers around the tree representing that season.

My girls love camping in the summer, and they adore winter sports. As for me, I love to bake once the weather gets cooler, and I always look forward to picking apples in the fall. We really enjoyed seeing the fun each season brings, so we hung our poster in the playroom. Some days it even plays a role in doll school!

Notes of Encouragement in Public Places

"No act of kindness, no matter how small, is ever wasted."
—Aesop

"The smallest act of kindness is worth more than the greatest intention."
—Kahlil Gibran

While teaching kids to express gratitude for their family and friends is one of the main points of this family project, giving back to the community, while more challenging, is almost as important. But with young kids, volunteer work is not always possible. That's why I looked for other ways in which my daughters and I could bring a smile to a stranger's face in our community.

So this family activity is all about that—making another mom in the park smile, helping other kids feel better about themselves, and encouraging people to spread the positivity by passing on these simple notes.

Since every local park, library, or even coffee shop usually has a place to hang announcements, we decided to hang notes of encouragement there. We chose our local park as it's our little neighborhood meeting place, with an ice rink in the winter and a splash pool in the summer. We also hung one at the bus stop, and then we brought one to the local library to hang on their announcements board.

ALL YOU NEED:
note of encouragement, printed

tape

1. Print the note out as many times as you want, available here: http://www.lazymoms blog.com/gratitude-printables.

2. On a sunny day, go on a stroll with your kids around your neighborhood and stick them to announcement boards in coffee shops or on poles in your local park. Ask your kids how they feel doing this, and how they think other people will feel when they'll notice the notes.

You can also get inspired by our note of encouragement and paint or draw one of your own. Whatever you choose, I hope it will be a great occasion to feel more connected to your community too!

Gratitude Quote for Kids' Rooms

Sometimes we all need a little reminder about the good things in life. This DIY gratitude quote is exactly that: It's a bright yet simple reminder that there's always something to be grateful for.

You can pick your favorite quote or help your child find one of their own. Here are a few examples:

💜 "There's always something to be thankful for."

💜 "Greet each day with a grateful heart."

💜 "Every day may not be good, but there's good in every day."

💜 "Choose to be grateful."

My six-year-old, Lili, chose the last one, mainly because it has the fewest letters!

ALL YOU NEED:

stencil letter stickers

small canvas or sheet of paper

sponge paint brush

paint

1. Place the stencil letters on the canvas or paper. Double check the spelling!

2. Carefully dip the sponge brush in a tiny amount of paint and paint inside the stencils. Don't worry if you paint outside the letter stencil, since it doesn't need to be perfect!

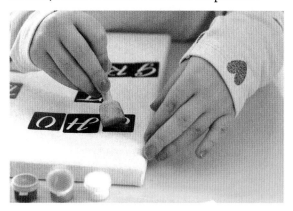

3. Once you're done, you can leave the space around white, or you can decorate it with dots or stars or even paint it too!

4. We chose to hang ours in the girls' bedroom. It's a great reminder that it's their choice to bring gratefulness into their lives.

If you feel that your kid may not have the patience necessary for carefully painting the letter stencils, you can use alphabet stickers. Simply stick the quote of your choice on your canvas or paper, and let your child paint over it with a large brush. Then, let it dry, and peel off the letters. It's a great way to help younger kids get involved in the craft or to make this activity easier for more impulsive kids!

Cookies in a Rainbow

You know we love baking and gifting our baked goods to family and friends, but we also love baking hacks! They make gifting even easier, especially if your little helpers are messy kitchen apprentices.

That's why for this activity you can either opt for store-bought cookies or you can bake your own oatmeal cookies. The "hack" for this project comes in at the end when it's time to decorate. Adding a bit of homemade goodness to store-bought cookies gives them a delicious and easy twist! We also tried to create the cutest, prettiest packaging for our cookies so that their appearance makes both the giver and the receiver happy. Cookies in a rainbow gifted on a gloomy fall afternoon are the perfect way to brighten anyone's day!

ALL YOU NEED:

cookies

milk or dark chocolate

sprinkles

colorful paper plates

pencil

scissors

tape

ribbon

1. First, "hack" your cookies. Start by melting the chocolate and preparing colorful sprinkles. Dip the cookies half in melted chocolate, and then generously sprinkle with sprinkles. Set aside.

2. Now prepare your packaging. Draw lines on the back of a paper plate as I did for guidance, and then cut only the edges.

3. Next, fold along the lines and secure with tape.

4. Wrap with a ribbon.

5. When the chocolate has hardened, put the cookies in the package and give it to someone who needs to be reminded of how grateful you are for them!

the Family Gratitude Project

If you'd like to bake oatmeal cookies like we did, here's our recipe:

INGREDIENTS:

2¼ cups quick-cooking rolled oats

⅔ cup unbleached all-purpose flour

pinch of salt

¾ cup softened butter

1 cup brown sugar

1 teaspoon vanilla extract

1 egg

2 bowls

mixer or spoon

1. Preheat the oven to 350°F.

2. Mix the oats, flour, and salt together in a bowl. Set aside.

3. Cream the butter with the sugar and vanilla in a separate bowl.

4. Mix the egg into the wet ingredients.

5. Add the dry ingredients to the wet slowly and stir with a mixer spoon. Combine well.

6. Use the spoon to place the dough on a cookie sheet, leaving about 2 inches between each one.

7. Bake for 12 to 15 minutes, until the edges become firm.

Family Gratitude Jar

November is a great month to start a family gratitude jar, especially if you're preparing to celebrate Thanksgiving with your family.

The concept of a gratitude jar is very simple. Every day for a month, each family member writes down on a piece of paper one thing that they feel grateful for that day. With the jar filling slowly day by day, kids can see the amount of gratefulness growing.

At the end of the month—or at Thanksgiving—read all the pieces of paper filled with stories and moments that brought gratitude.

ALL YOU NEED:

large jar

decorative ribbons or jute tape

glue

label

pen

crafting paper

scissors

small bowl or a glass

1. Start by decorating the jar. We used adhesive jute tape that's very easy to stick on, as well as a ribbon.

2. Now it's time to add a label. You can simply write "Gratitude Jar," or you can add your family's name too.

3. Next, cut out small pieces of crafting paper and place them on a bowl or in a small glass near the jar. Don't forget to add a pen!

4. Place the family gratitude jar on the table where you eat most of your family meals together, and let the jar fill up with stories and memories of your family's thankfulness.

My two daughters loved having this new mealtime ritual, and even though my younger one can't write just yet, it was her who was reminding us every day to "do the jar!" When it was time to read them all aloud, it was the sweetest family experience.

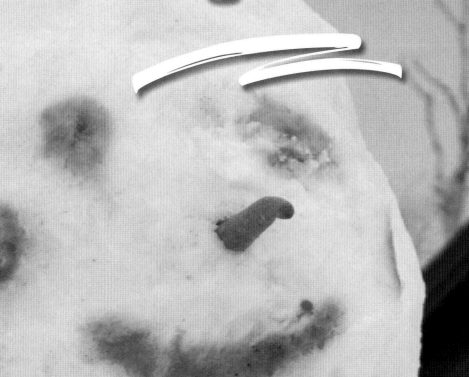

Winter Projects

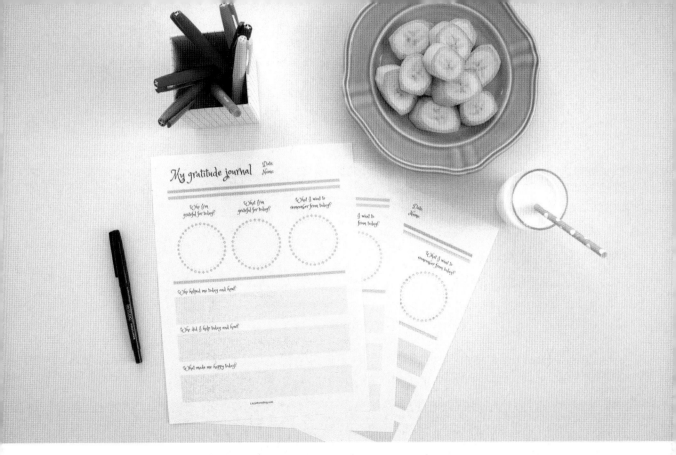

Printable Gratitude Journal

Journaling is a great way to gain insight for adults and can also be a fun activity for kids. By helping kids remember all the little things that made them feel happy, sad, or thankful and by letting them reconnect with their feelings, they can feel better and more grateful in their everyday lives.

Since only one of my daughters is in school and has just started to read and write, and my second daughter is currently four and definitely can't write just yet, I created two different sets of journaling pages. One is for the school-aged kids, and one is for toddlers and preschoolers. Find them here: http://www.lazymomsblog.com/gratitude-printables.

The journaling pages for school-aged kids are a great year-round activity, but can be especially meaningful during the weeks preceding Thanksgiving and the winter holidays. You can print them at home and fill out one each day for a month, or just one a week, whatever rhythm fits your child better.

The draw-in journaling pages for preschoolers or toddlers, have four simple questions with space to draw their answers. Of course, younger kids might need more guidance and encouragement, but their answers might be surprising and funny!

Sometimes, our youngest kids can teach us that it's the littlest things that matter the most to them—like a sister who pours them milk in the morning.

If you don't have access to a printer or a computer, no problem! Simply use scrap paper or an old notebook. You can copy the questions below onto the page using a colorful pen, pencil, or crayon. Just make sure to leave space for your child's answers!

- Who I'm grateful for today:
- What I'm grateful for today:
- What I want to remember from today:
- Who helped me today and how:
- Who did I help today and how:
- What made me happy today:

Salt Dough Medals

One of the very first crafts I have ever made with my firstborn was salt dough. I think she must have been 18 months old when we made it together for the first time! And since it's super easy to make, affordable, and versatile, it's a staple of rainy-day activities in our home. Toddlers love playing with it and older children love making things from it.

These salt dough medals are not only a great way to pass time on a snowy day, but they also help kids realize who is important to them and why are they grateful for that person's presence. You can make "#1 Dad," "Super-cousin," "Best Grandma" medals, and more!

ALL YOU NEED:

cookie sheet

parchment paper

½ cup flour

¼ cup cornstarch

¼ cup salt

medium bowl

3 tablespoons warm water

round cookie cutter or small glass

toothpicks

acrylic crafting paint

paint brushes

ribbon

1. Preheat the oven to 350°F and line a cookie sheet with parchment paper.

2. Mix the flour, cornstarch, and salt together in the medium bowl, then add the water.

3. Using your hands, knead the dough. If it's too dry, add a little bit more water (not more than 1 teaspoon at a time). If it's too sticky, add more flour and salt (again, not more than 1 teaspoon at a time).

4. Once it's smooth and easy to roll in a ball, it's ready!

5. Divide the dough into two parts and roll out each half. If it sticks to your work surface, sprinkle the table with flour.

6. Cut out the medals using a round cookie cutter or a small glass.

7. Place the medals on to the parchment paper-lined cookie sheet. Make holes in each medal with a toothpick. Remember that you want your medals to hang, so try to place the holes off center and close to the edge, but not too close, so they won't fall apart. Bake for about 20 minutes.

8. Once the medals completely cool down, it's time to paint them! It's up to your kids if they want to write a short appreciation note on the back side. They can also write a "#1" on the front like we did. What's important is that kids get to express their appreciation and gratitude for the people around them!

9. Thread ribbon through the holes of the medals once the paint is completely dry.

Paper Chain of Gratitude

When I was growing up in Poland, my mom and I used to make handmade Christmas tree decorations each December. Some years we would paint pine cones in gold, others we would dry orange slices and hang them on the Christmas tree, and some years we would make long paper chains just like this one.

The beauty of this paper chain lies in its simplicity—it can be made out of white paper for a minimalistic "Scandinavian" look, or it can be from thick colorful cardstock for a more festive look. It can hang on a Christmas tree or can add a subtle touch of Christmas decor in kids' rooms above their beds.

It's great for gratitude practicing too, because after it's all done, we can talk with kids about family and community, and how everyone is connected with someone, how alone we can struggle, but together we're so much stronger, just like a chain.

ALL YOU NEED:

2 colors craft paper

scissors

markers or pens

glue

the Family Gratitude Project

1. First, cut long strips from both colors of paper. If you prefer a delicate chain, measure 2 inches long and about ½ inch wide. But if you'd like a larger chain like we did, measure at least 4 inches long and 1 inch wide.

2. Help your children think about who they are thankful for this week. What little blessings are they grateful for? Who in your community is important to your kids? Write their names on the reverse side of the paper stripes. Their names will form the chain of gratitude.

3. Now, glue two edges of a paper strip together to form a circle. Then, add the second one of a different color, interlocking it with the first. Continue until you're out of strips and your chain is complete.

4. Hang it on the Christmas tree, on the fireplace mantel, or above the bed.

Gratitude Charades

Did you like playing charades growing up? It used to be one of my favorite camp games, where without any equipment and lots of imagination, we would have fun for hours.

If you haven't tried playing charades with your kids, I think now is the time! Kids love seeing their parents and family members getting silly, and it's a great game to play during the long winter evenings when all the toys are already boring and screen time is over.

This spin on charades is about acting out and guessing what each person is grateful for this week: Is it an object? A person? An event?

HOW TO PLAY:

💜 Make sure that you have at least four people, although it's best to be a group of six to ten family members.

💜 Divide your family into two teams, preferably with the same number of adults and kids on each team.

💜 Members of team A (and then, in the next round, the members of team B) need to guess what their representative is trying to show using only gestures and their own body, but without words or props; they can also draw what they're grateful for on a dry-erase board, but without using words.

💜 There should be as many rounds as there are members in each team so each member has a chance to perform and show their gratitude.

💜 The team that guesses the most wins. They should be rewarded with cookies!

💜 I'm sure your family will love playing gratitude charades as much as mine did!

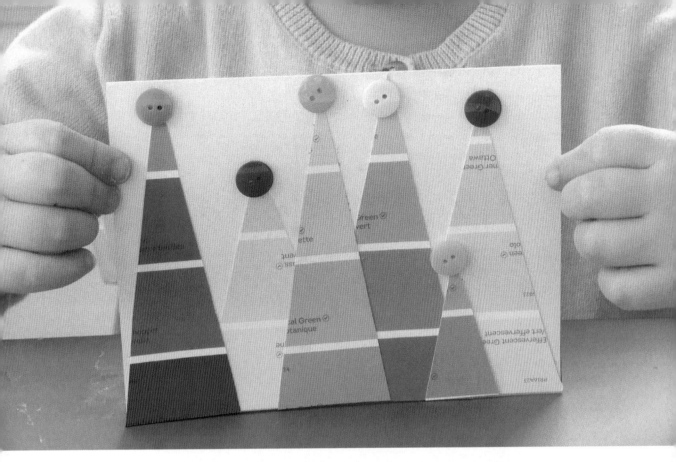

DIY Christmas Cards

This DIY Christmas thank-you card is a perfect craft to make on a cold December afternoon, and easy enough that even toddlers can partake in the fun. Plus, it's festive enough to be sent as a holiday card to family and friends.

My youngest daughter is four, so she knows how to use her little scissors. She was so happy making these cards on her own, and all the while she got to practice both gratitude and fine motor skills—that's what I call a mom win!

ALL YOU NEED:

green paint swatches of different shades

scissors

white craft paper or blank, ready-to-use cards

glue

adhesive buttons or regular buttons

1. First, prepare the Christmas trees. Simply cut long triangles of different sizes from the green paint swatches.

2. Cut a rectangle for the card out of the craft paper.

3. Glue the Christmas trees on the white card. Help your child arrange the triangles so that there are different sizes and shades of green touching each other.

4. Finally, add little colorful buttons on top of the Christmas trees as decoration.

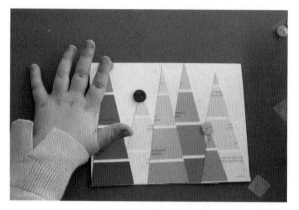

And that's it, your winter DIY card is ready. See, even a toddler can make it! Now all that's left to do is send them to all of your family and friends with the warmest season's wishes. I'm sure they'll feel grateful for your labor of love.

DIY Snow Spray

Being grateful for nature is something I think we all have as kids but tend to lose as adults. As grownups we tend to move through life without really appreciating the world around us. So this simple DIY is more of a family activity, and a great way to enjoy snow with your kids even if you're the type of person who'd rather cuddle underneath the blankets instead!

This snow spray is also a great idea for climates where you might not get enough snow to make a snowman or snow fort. All you need is just enough fresh powder on the ground in order to write messages and draw doodles!

We used our snow spray for painting our snowman's face, since finding rocks for the eyes and mouth is always a struggle. This spray made building our snowman so much easier and more fun! Lili sprayed his eyes, mouth, and even some buttons and then decided that from now on this is the only right way to make a snowman. We also used our snow spray to make colorful snowballs that add a bright pop to any snowball fight!

ALL YOU NEED:

water

food coloring of choice

small spray bottles

Simply mix water and a couple drops of each color of food coloring in spray bottles and shake, shake, shake!

That's it! Now you have your own snow spray that's much cheaper than the store-bought kind.

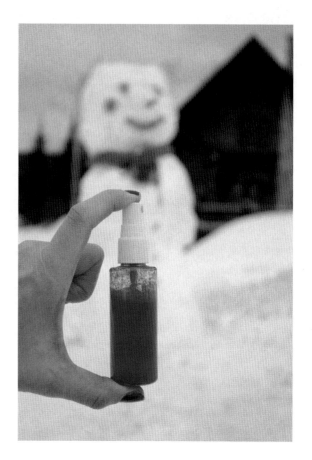

the Family Gratitude Project

Valentine's Day Garland

Celebrating Valentine's Day with kids usually ends up with everyone eating way too many heart-shaped candies and signing too many Valentine's cards! Well, I won't tell you to get rid of all the candy, but I promise that this craft will leave you feeling better and your kids more grateful.

This "all the people I love" garland helps kids realize how many people they love and care for. It's perfect to make before Valentine's Day, as it becomes a cute and colorful decoration with meaning. My daughter loved having the garland above her bed. During bedtime, she'd name everyone that she loves, and would show me the hearts and guess the letters. I think for a four-year-old, that's pretty close to gratefulness!

ALL YOU NEED:

colorful sheets of paper

heart-shaped cookie cutter

pen

scissors

rope

small crafting clothespins

1. Start by folding a sheet of paper in half, and then in half again. Next, using a heart-shaped cookie cutter, draw a heart in the middle of the folded paper.

2. Cut the hearts out. You'll be cutting out four hearts at once! Repeat steps 1 and 2 until you have at least 12 colorful paper hearts.

3. Now it's time to hang these little hearts on the rope. The clothespins make this very easy for little hands, and they are also great for helping kids practice their fine motor skills. (You can also tie the hearts to the string if you prefer.)

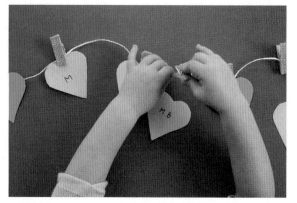

4. Once the garland is assembled, it's time for the most important part: naming the people who are dear to your child's heart. My daughter felt her heart grow once she named everyone that she loves. After you have the list of loved ones, write their initials on the hearts.

5. Finally, hang the garland above your child's bed so they can look at it every night before going to sleep.

Valentine's Cookies

As much as my kids and I love to craft, we also love to bake. There's nothing quite as comforting on a cold and snowy or a dark and rainy afternoon than making your home smell like cookies. And there's not much that makes a person smile more than a gift of home-baked goods. So to help my kids make their friends smile, we bake these buttery, crunchy sugar cookies, which are really amazing once covered with pink cream cheese icing!

FOR THE COOKIES:

¾ cup softened butter

¾ cup granulated sugar

1 large egg

2 teaspoons vanilla extract

2¼ cups flour

large bowl

rolling pin

heart-shaped cookie cutter

FOR THE CREAM CHEESE ICING:

electric mixer or hand mixer

1 cup cream cheese, at room temperature

2½ cups icing sugar

2 tablespoons milk, at room temperature

several small bowls and spoons

pink food coloring

YIELD: *About 18 to 24 cookies*

1. Mix together the butter, sugar, egg, and vanilla extract in a large bowl.

2. Add the flour and mix well.

3. Roll the dough in a ball, cover, and refrigerate for 1 hour.

4. Preheat the oven to 350°F.

5. Remove the dough from the fridge, cut a thick slice of the dough from the rest, and roll it out. While you're not using the rest of dough, put it back in the fridge.

6. Cut out the cookies with a heart-shaped cookie cutter. Place on a cookie sheet and bake for about 10 to 12 minutes, until golden. Remove from the oven and let cool. Repeat with the remaining dough.

7. To make the icing, use an electric stand mixer or hand mixer to combine the room temperature cream cheese with the icing sugar and milk. Mix until very smooth.

8. Now, divide your icing between the small bowls, one for each color. Add one drop of pink food coloring to the first bowl and mix it well with a spoon. Very slowly increase the quantity of food coloring until you achieve the shade you're happy with. Do this with each bowl of icing. I like to have a variety of shades of pink!

9. Once the cookies have cooled, it's time to put on the icing. We used a teaspoon, but of course you can use a pastry bag if you prefer.

10. After the icing sets and hardens slightly, you can pack up your cookies and gift them!

the Family Gratitude Project

Thankful Salt Dough Hearts

One of our favorite spring celebrations is Valentine's Day, but many kids associate this holiday with only one thing—chocolate! This craft is a fun way to remind your kids what Valentine's Day is really about: appreciation for the people we love. It's a day to celebrate love of all kinds, so I try to help my kids not only acknowledge who they love, but also why they are grateful for having these people in their lives.

Making these salt dough hearts is a great activity to create a conversation about all the people that your child loves. Then, once the hearts are done, kids can give them to all their loved ones. Just make sure to let your loved ones know that, while these hearts might look good enough to eat, they're only for decoration!

But of course, you don't need to wait for Valentine's Day to celebrate all the people that you love with your child. This activity would be fun to make any time of the year!

ALL YOU NEED:

2 teaspoons strawberry gelatin powder

2 cups flour

¾ cup salt

1 cup warm water

medium bowl

spoon

rolling pin

heart-shaped cookie cutter

1. Let your child combine all of the ingredients in a medium bowl and stir until a dough is formed. It should be easy to work with—not too sticky or too tough.

2. If the mixture is too sticky, add more flour and salt, and if it's not sticky enough add more warm water. The gelatin is a great and easy way to add color. You can add more or less gelatin powder depending on how saturated you want the color to be.

3. Roll out the dough on the kitchen table or counter until it's around half a centimeter thick.

4. Cut out the hearts using a cookie cutter.

5. Let the hearts dry for around 24 hours in a cool, dry place, or bake them in the oven for around 10 minutes at 350°F.

6. Once the hearts are all cooled down or dried out, they're ready to be given to family and friends!

DIY Clay Dishes

With Christmas approaching, you might be asking yourself what easy DIY gifts you could make with your kids this year (or if you weren't just yet, I bet I got you thinking about this now!). These clay dishes make for a perfect ring holder gift for any grandma, auntie, or family friend. And if you make them a bit bigger you can call them individual cookie plates, and then they make for a perfect gift for anyone!

And what's better for expressing gratitude than making a homemade gift for a loved one? Nothing, really!

The best part is that these clay ring holders are absolutely doable for kids and very inexpensive.

ALL YOU NEED:

package of air-drying clay	knife
pin roller	paint
several bowls of different sizes	paint brushes

1. First, cut the clay into four or five smaller chunks, and roll it piece by piece until each is around ¼ inch thick.

2. Then, place a small bowl upside down on top of a piece of clay, and cut a circle around the edges using your bowl as a form. You can play with sizes, and make some dishes smaller and some bigger. Make sure to watch your children carefully as they cut out the circles, or do this part yourself!

3. You can leave them simple or decorate the edges with small lines using a plastic knife. You can even make a fancy ring holder with a simple bird or cat shape glued with water to the center of your dish.

4. To let them dry, place them inside bowls; depending on the size of the bowl they might dry to be more or less flat.

the Family Gratitude Project

5. Let them dry completely before painting; it might take a couple of days or up to a week. Once dried, paint them all white, all gold, or all black—or in the colors of the rainbow. Just remember that they are quite fragile.

6. Pack the dishes in small boxes and gift them! You might want to keep one for yourself though. They are really cute and so useful!

Sparkly Sensory Bottle

Sensory activities are a great way to entertain a distractible toddler, and they're also a fun way to capture the attention of kids of all ages. This sparkly sensory bottle is really easy and fun to put together, and is a great way to reconnect with feelings of gratefulness.

ALL YOU NEED:

empty plastic bottle

water, at room temperature

glitter paint

craft glitter, as needed

cooking oil or baby oil

small objects like beads, confetti, or tiny colorful rocks

glue

family photo

washi tape

1. Fill the plastic bottle one-third of the way full with room-temperature water.

2. Add a teaspoon of glitter paint of your choice (if it's not sparkly enough, add some craft glitter too).

3. Fill up the rest of the bottle with oil.

4. Add small objects like colorful beads, plastic confetti, or tiny rocks.

5. Finally, glue on the lid so it doesn't leak!

6. Now cut out a family photo that evokes memories of happiness and family fun, and stick it on the bottle with washi tape.

Once the bottle is done, encourage your kids to tell you a story about the moment that was captured in the photo. Ask them if they remember how they felt that day, what they did right after the photo was taken, and what smells accompanied that moment.

Ask them what they feel now when they think about that moment. Are they grateful for what happened or the people that helped make those fond memories?

The next time your child gets sad or angry, they can shake their sparkly bottle, watch the glitter and beads swirling, and remember the happy moments from the photograph. This is a great way to help your child calm down.

Chocolate Chip and
Oatmeal Cookies

Preheat the oven to 350 degrees and
prepare a baking sheet.
Pour the contents of the jar in a large
bowl and mix with 1/2 cup melted
butter, 1 egg and 1/2 teaspoon
vanilla extract.
Roll cookies into 1/2 inch balls,
place on the prepared baking sheet
and bake for 10 minutes. Enjoy!

Chocolate Chip and Oatmeal Cookies in a Jar

One of the great ways for kids to show their gratitude and appreciation is by making these edible gifts for family and friends. What we love about cookies in a jar is that they are easy to prepare, and many of these ingredients are already in our pantry. And while kids get to assemble the cookies in a jar, they don't get to taste them, unlike when we bake cookies for family and friends and we do "quality control," aka we eat one-third of all the cookies! When kids prepare cookies in a jar, they get to do something entirely for someone else—and the only gratification is a smile and a hug. Which, if you ask me, is the best! So to encourage kids to give back and gift their family members and neighbors, we make these chocolate chip and oatmeal cookies in a jar!

ALL YOU NEED:

1⅓ cups all-purpose flour, spooned into a measuring cup and leveled

1 teaspoon baking powder

1 teaspoon baking soda

¼ teaspoon salt

medium bowl

1-quart mason jar

1 cup quick-cooking oats; if you prefer crispier cookies, use old-fashioned oats

1 cup semisweet chocolate chips

½ cup light brown sugar, packed

½ cup granulated sugar

1. First, stir the flour, baking powder, baking soda, and salt together in a bowl.

2. Pour this mixture into a 1-quart mason jar and level.

3. Now add the oats.

4. Pour the chocolate chips on top of the oats.

5. Finally, add the brown sugar and the granulated sugar on top. Close the jar tightly, and voilà!

I have made a printable with baking instructions for you, that you can print from http://www.lazymomsblog.com/gratitude-printables. You can also write the instructions by hand! If you choose the printable, simply cut it out and stick on the jar.

And, if you prefer to give a gift with your kid's handwriting, here are the instructions.

Chocolate Chip and Oatmeal Cookies

Preheat the oven to 350°F and prepare a baking sheet with parchment paper.

Pour the contents of the jar into a large bowl and mix with ½ cup melted butter, 1 egg, and ½ teaspoon vanilla extract.

Roll the cookies into ½-inch balls, place on the prepared baking sheet, and bake for 10 minutes. Enjoy!

Of course, nothing prevents you from making one of these pantry staples for your family too—they are so yummy!

Helpful Hands Wreath

One of the important components of gratitude is recognizing what others do to help us in our everyday lives. This craft is all about that! First, kids get to identify moments when someone gave them a helpful hand. Then, they get to tell the story of how it helped them. Finally, they write down the name of the person, and they keep the wreath as a reminder of all the people who were there for them.

This craft really helped my daughters realize that every helpful act, no matter how big or small, is something to be grateful for. Whether it's a friend who lends them a pencil when theirs is broken, or whether it's learning to ski in the cold with their dad, sometimes my kids might take these things for granted.

That's why this craft is so fun. Not only does it look adorable hanging in a kid's room, but it's also a visual reminder of all the helping hands they've gotten.

ALL YOU NEED:

4 sheets of colorful paper

colorful paint

scissors

pencil

glue

string (optional)

1. Start by having your kid stamp his or her handprints with the paint onto the paper. Use a variety of color combinations!

2. Let the handprints dry, and then let your child cut them out.

3. Draw an imperfect wreath on another piece of paper and cut it out.

4. Now it's time to glue the handprints on. There's no right way—the handprints can all point in the same direction, or they can be glued in pairs.

5. Now ask your child to tell you who gave him or her a helping hand this week and in what way it was helpful. Encourage them to tell a story and help them see how sometimes people don't have to help them but do so anyway. On each handprint, write a name of someone who lent your child a helping hand.

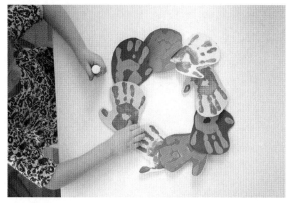

6. Hang the finished wreath (use string if needed) in a place where your child can see it and be reminded of all the people who are there for them. Now that's something to feel grateful for!

If your kid can't come up with ideas, ask them if they were helped by a family member or a friend at school. For instance, did someone help them with their homework or clean up after a playdate?

Giving Back as a Family

Congratulations on coming to the end of this book of gratitude projects! As you continue on in your journey of bringing gratitude and thankfulness into your family's lifestyle, here's a list of other ways in which you can give back as a family. Some of these activities take more time and effort, while others can easily become a part of your routine.

- Sort through toys and clothes and donate to your local Salvation Army, local help center, or shelters.

- Sort canned food and donate to the local food pantry.

- Pick up trash and litter at a local park or playground.

- Volunteer as a family at a local food pantry (with kids over 12 years old).

- Make bathroom kits for shelters.

- Offer to be a mother's helper team for a new mom in the neighborhood.

- Help in a soup kitchen.

- Sponsor a child through a charity program.

- Make micro-loans with your kids' piggy bank money through an organization like KIVA (www.kiva.org).

- Volunteer at a local animal shelter.

- Hold a bake sale or lemonade stand to raise money for charity.

- Pack up boxes for Operation Christmas Child.

- Do yard work for a neighbor.

- Donate books to a local library.

- Participate in a run for a good cause.

- Walk your neighbor's dog.

- Pay for a family behind you in a drive-through.

- Shovel a neighbor's driveway on a snow day.

- Babysit for free.

- Leave change in a vending machine.

Conversion Charts

Volume Conversions

U.S.	U.S. Equivalent	Metric
1 tablespoon (3 teaspoons)	½ fluid ounce	15 milliliters
¼ cup	2 fluid ounces	60 milliliters
⅓ cup	3 fluid ounces	90 milliliters
½ cup	4 fluid ounces	120 milliliters
⅔ cup	5 fluid ounces	150 milliliters
¾ cup	6 fluid ounces	180 milliliters
1 cup	8 fluid ounces	240 milliliters
2 cups	16 fluid ounces	480 milliliters

Weight Conversions

U.S.	Metric
½ ounce	15 grams
1 ounce	30 grams
2 ounces	60 grams
¼ pound	115 grams
⅓ pound	150 grams
½ pound	225 grams
¾ pound	350 grams
1 pound	450 grams

Temperature Conversions

Fahrenheit (°F)	Celsius (°C)	Fahrenheit (°F)	Celsius (°C)
70°F	20°C	220°F	105°C
100°F	40°C	240°F	115°C
120°F	50°C	260°F	125°C
130°F	55°C	280°F	140°C
140°F	60°C	300°F	150°C
150°F	65°C	325°F	165°C
160°F	70°C	350°F	175°C
170°F	75°C	375°F	190°C
180°F	80°C	400°F	200°C
190°F	90°C	425°F	220°C
200°F	95°C	450°F	230°C

the Family Gratitude Project

Acknowledgments

A huge thank you to Casie Vogel for believing in me and to Claire Sielaff for helping me throughout the process.

Thank you to my patient husband who has been supporting me all the way.

And thank you to my mom for crafting with me when I was little—dziękuje ci Mamo!

About the Author

Joanna Grzeszczak (pronounced Gshe-sh-ch-ak) was born and raised in Poland and earned a master's degree in psychology, with a focus on family, in 2008 at the University of Wroclaw. Shortly after, at the age of 25, she moved to Montreal, Canada, where she pursued her studies at the University of Montreal and earned a certificate in French language. She now lives with her French-speaking husband, Vincent, two daughters, Lilianne and Mila-Rose, and baby, Julien, in a small city cottage.

Valerie Gay-Bessette

She started writing and photographing in 2014, and has established herself as a blogger and content creator on the *Lazy Mom's Blog*. Her work is centered around mindful living, family lifestyle, and home decorating, and her mission is to inspire and uplift others on this difficult journey of motherhood. Her articles on self-help, positive body image, and parenting have been widely shared throughout social media, and her decorating projects have been featured in furniture catalogs and *Canadian Living* magazine. But the core of her blog has always been raising kids, crafting with them, and finding creative ways to help them develop independent thinking, imagination, and gratitude. When she doesn't write or photograph, she can be found in the kitchen baking cookies with her kids or redecorating someone's home.